Ultimate Science Lab

EXPERIMENTS with LIVING THINGS

Anna Claybourne

T0018333

Gareth Stevens
PUBLISHING

Please visit our website, www.garethstevens.com. For a free color catalog of all our high-quality books, call toll free 1-800-542-2595 or fax 1-877-542-2596.

Cataloging-in-Publication Data

Names: Claybourne, Anna.
Title: Experiments with living things / Anna Claybourne.
Description: New York : Gareth Stevens Publishing, 2019. | Series: Ultimate science lab | Includes glossary and index.
Identifiers: ISBN 9781538235508 (pbk.) | ISBN 9781538235522 (library bound) | ISBN 9781538235515 (6pack)
Subjects: LCSH: Biology--Experiments--Juvenile literature. | Plants--Experiments--Juvenile literature.
Classification: LCC QH316.5 C5725 2019 | DDC 570.72'4--dc23

First Edition

Published in 2019 by
Gareth Stevens Publishing
111 East 14th Street, Suite 349
New York, NY 10003

Copyright © Arcturus Holdings Ltd, 2019

Author: Anna Claybourne
Science consultant: Thomas Canavan
Experiment illustrations: Jessica Secheret
Other illustrations: Richard Watson
Photos: Shutterstock
Design: Supriya Sahai, with Emma Randall
Editor: Joe Fullman, with Julia Adams

Printed in the United States of America

CPSIA compliance information: Batch #CW19GS: For further information contact Gareth Stevens, New York, New York at 1-800-542-2595.

CONTENTS

START EXPERIMENTING!

This book is packed with exciting experiments that train your pets, grow plants, or are so incredible you won't believe your eyes! But there's nothing magical in these pages—it's all real-life amazing **SCIENCE**.

BE ECO-FRIENDLY!

First things first. As scientists, we aim to be as environmentally friendly as possible. Experiments require lots of different materials, including plastic ones, so we need to make sure we reuse and recycle as much as we can ...

* Some experiments use plastic straws; rather than buying a large amount, ask in coffee shops or restaurants whether they can spare a few for your experiments.

* Old cereal boxes are great for experiments that use cardboard.

* Save old school worksheets and other paper you no longer need, to reuse for experiments.

WHAT YOU'LL NEED

You can do most of these experiments with everyday items you'll find around the house.

Some useful things to have handy are ...

* Paper and cardboard
* Pens and pencils
* String
* Glue
* Tape
* Straws (plastic ones are best)
* Plates, bowls, jugs, and plastic food containers
* Scissors
* Rubber bands
* Paper cups
* Balloons

STAY SAFE!

Experiments are fun, but some of them can be dangerous if they're not done carefully ... so don't forget these safety tips:

✸ You will need an adult to help with experiments that involve cooking and heating, matches and candles, and sharp cutting tools. Wherever an experiment has something like this in it, you'll see this sign to remind you:

> ⊘ **ASK AN ADULT!**

✸ Follow all the instructions carefully to make sure you use all the equipment and materials in a safe way.

✸ If an experiment requires you to stand on a chair, make sure you have someone to assist you. Check the that chair is placed in a stable position and ask the person helping you to hold the chair while you are using it.

✹ Stand back from anything that's moving fast, or that involves eruptions or explosions. And don't throw, shoot, or whirl things around unless you're completely sure there's no one nearby.

And remember...

Always do experiments somewhere that's easy to clean up, like a kitchen or bathroom—NOT on the fancy carpet! And make sure you do clean up after yourself. Some of these experiments are messy!

So, are you ready to see some science? Step this way ...

LIVING EXPERIMENTS

Studying living things is a huge part of science. Life is all around us—trees, grass, germs, pets, farm animals, and wildlife—and we ourselves are alive, too! Living things, including the human body, work in all kinds of amazing ways.

WHAT IS LIFE?
So what makes something alive? Here's a list of things that all living things do. If it doesn't do all these things, it's not alive!

Move
Respond to its environment (though some other things move, too, such as waves or clouds).

Grow
Start off smaller and get bigger.

Respire
Make energy from food, usually using gases from the air.

Eat
Take in food of some kind.

Sense
Detect things around it, using its senses.

Reproduce
Make copies of itself—by having babies, for example.

Excrete
Let out waste. For example, there are waste gases in the breath you breathe out.

Hands in the air

Try this quick and easy experiment to show how blood carries oxygen to your muscles. You need two arms, two hands, and a timer.

Set the timer going, then put one arm straight up in the air, and the other down by your side. Start opening and closing both your hands as fast as you can, making a star shape, then a fist, and repeating.

How long can you keep this going? As time goes on, do your hands start to feel different from each other? Can you keep them both moving at the same speed—or do you have to stop moving one a bit sooner than the other?

HOW DOES IT WORK?

Muscle cells use oxygen to make energy, so that your body can move. Sticking your hand up makes it hard for enough blood to get uphill to the muscles to deliver the oxygen needed to keep the hand moving. When the muscles run short of oxygen, they release a chemical called lactic acid to help them make energy—but this only works for a while, and is quite painful. So your hand hurts and wants to stop moving. The other hand is still getting lots of blood, so it can keep going!

SEEDS ON A SOCK

Look at Earth from space, and you'll see a LOT of green. It's all the plants! Plants can spread over large areas using seeds, which can get carried long distances by wind, water, or animals. And that includes you!

WHAT YOU'LL NEED:

* ★ A large, old, unwanted sock
* ★ Somewhere wild to go for a walk, such as a forest, hill, or park
* ★ Scissors
* ★ An old cardboard box, such as a shoebox
* ★ Potting compost (from a garden center or supermarket)

⚠ ASK AN ADULT!

1. First, get an adult to agree to take you for a walk, somewhere with lots of plants. Before you set off, pull an old sock over one of your shoes. An adult's sock is best, as it will fit over your shoe more easily.

You'll probably get the best results in summer or fall, when plants are making the most seeds.

2. Go for your walk with the sock on. When you get home, take the sock off, and use the scissors to cut along one side, so that it opens out flat.

3. Put a shallow layer of compost in the bottom of your box, then lay the opened-out sock on top, muddy side up.

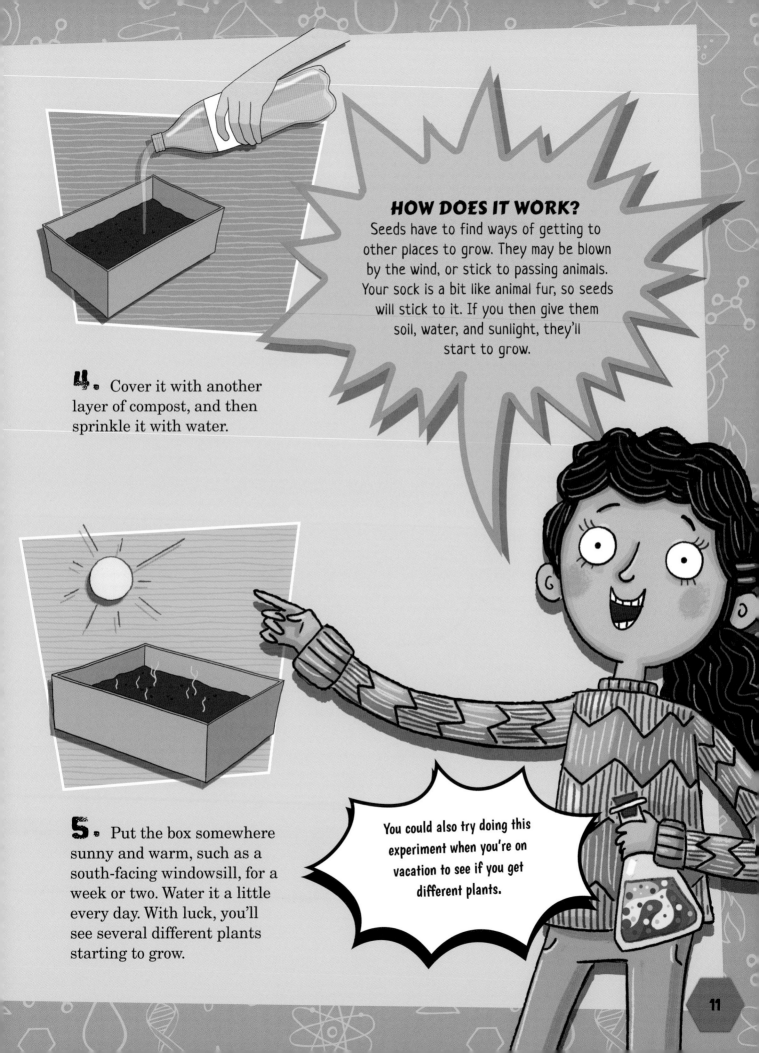

HOW DOES IT WORK?

Seeds have to find ways of getting to other places to grow. They may be blown by the wind, or stick to passing animals. Your sock is a bit like animal fur, so seeds will stick to it. If you then give them soil, water, and sunlight, they'll start to grow.

4. Cover it with another layer of compost, and then sprinkle it with water.

5. Put the box somewhere sunny and warm, such as a south-facing windowsill, for a week or two. Water it a little every day. With luck, you'll see several different plants starting to grow.

You could also try doing this experiment when you're on vacation to see if you get different plants.

STICKY SLIME

Snails and slugs leave silvery, slimy trails wherever they go. Have you ever wondered what that slimy stuff is, and what's it for? This is an experiment to try in a park or garden in spring or summer.

WHAT YOU'LL NEED:
* ★ A plastic tray or large plastic plate
* ★ A snail and a slug (most yards have plenty)
* ★ Lettuce, apple, or cucumber as food
* ★ 2 paper clips
* ★ 2 small coins

You can pick slugs and snails up with your fingers, as long as you wash your hands afterward. But if you don't want to touch them, you could wear rubber gloves.

1. First, find some snails and slugs. Look around plants and under leaves. They especially like vegetable plants. If you can't find a slug and a snail, just one of them will do. Be sure to handle them gently.

2. Put your slug and snail at one side of your tray or plate. Encourage them to move across it by placing food in front of them (it could take a while!).

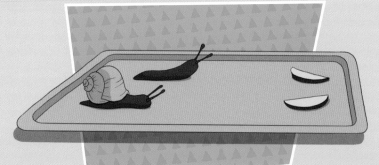

3. Put the slug and snail back where you found them. Now test their slime. Do the two trails look different from each other?

4. Try sticking a piece of food, a paper clip, and a coin to each slime trail, then slowly turning the tray or plate upside down to see if they stay on. How sticky is the slime? Is one trail stickier than the other?

A plain plate or tray, with no patterns, will make it easier to see the slime!

HOW DOES IT WORK?

Snail and slug slime is a gel made of a stringy substance mixed with other chemicals. It lets snails and slugs glide more easily over rough surfaces. It's also very sticky, helping them to slither up plant stems, walls, and flowerpots. And it kills germs and protects the snail or slug's skin—which is why it's sometimes used to make beauty creams!

PAVLOV'S PETS

Russian scientist Ivan Pavlov did a famous experiment on dogs to study how they learn. It's easy to try at home if you have a dog or cat. Don't worry, it's harmless!

WHAT YOU'LL NEED:
* A pet dog or cat
* Their regular food
* A bell, duck squeaker, or something else that makes an unusual noise

Your bell or other noisemaker should be something the animal hasn't heard before. An unusual smartphone alarm tone should also work.

1. To do this experiment, you need your cat or dog to link the new sound with being fed. Every time they are just about to be fed, make the noise a few times. (Make sure the noise isn't too loud, or you might scare them.)

Don't make the noise at any other time except feeding time, as this could confuse your pet and the experiment won't work.

2. After a few days, make the noise just before feeding time, but without having any food ready. If it's worked, they should still come running for their food.

3. You could try more tests. Does one pet learn more quickly than another? Does it work on pet guinea pigs, hamsters, or fish? Can you link a different sound to going for a walk, or playing with a toy?

HOW DOES IT WORK?

In his experiments, Pavlov found that dogs drooled and dribbled when they saw food. He rang a bell at feeding time, and eventually the dogs would drool whenever they heard the bell, even if there was no food around. The experiment shows how animals can learn by connecting unrelated things together in their brains. If your cat or dog runs in expecting to be fed when it hears the noise, you can tell the experiment has worked.

TWO-POINT TOUCH TEST

This is an experiment for you and friends or family to try on each other. You might think your skin can tell the difference between one touch and two—but it's not that simple!

WHAT YOU'LL NEED:
* Paper clips
* A ruler
* A pencil and paper
* At least two people

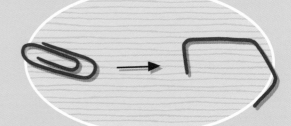

1. Open out a paper clip and bend it into a rough "U" shape, like this. The two ends should be lined up and pointing the same way.

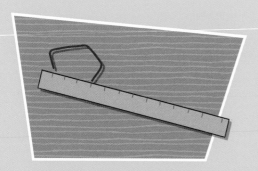

2. Use the ruler to measure the distance between the ends of the paper clip, and write it down.

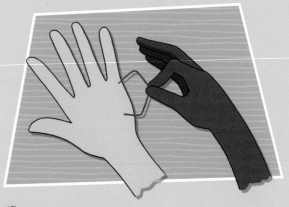

3. To do the test, the person being tested should sit down and close their eyes, while the tester uses the paper clip to gently press on their skin. Start with the palm of the hand. Ask if the person can feel one point, or two.

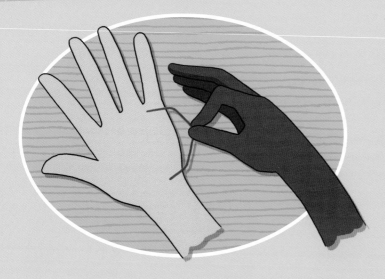

4. If they can only feel one, move the ends farther apart, measure them again, and try again. If they can feel two, move the ends closer together, and try again.

5. Sometimes, at random, just press one end of the paper clip onto the skin. This makes sure the person being tested really can tell the difference between one and two points.

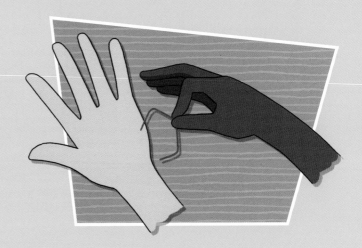

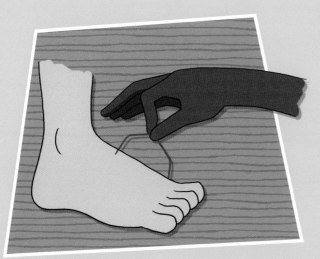

6. Repeat the experiment on these different parts of the body:
• Top of the foot
• Calf
• Fingertip
• Cheek
• Shoulder

Write down how far apart the ends of the paper clip have to be before the person can feel two points instead of one. For example, on the back of the hand, it might be a ½ inch (12 mm).

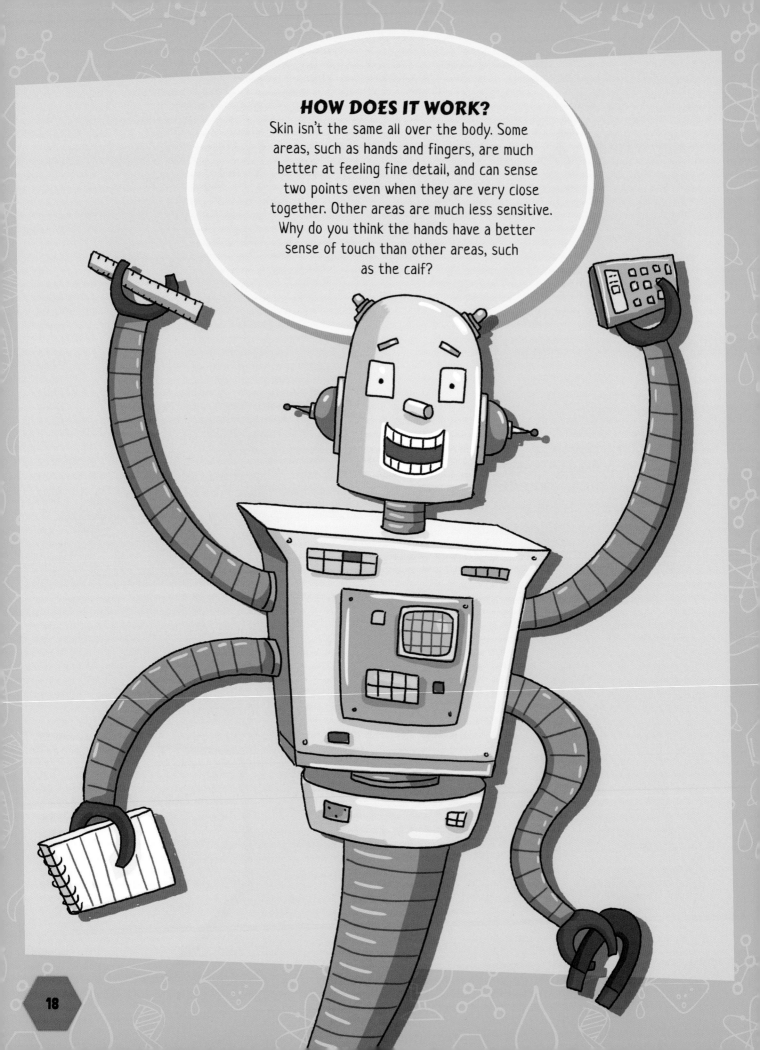

HOW DOES IT WORK?

Skin isn't the same all over the body. Some areas, such as hands and fingers, are much better at feeling fine detail, and can sense two points even when they are very close together. Other areas are much less sensitive. Why do you think the hands have a better sense of touch than other areas, such as the calf?

SEEING IS BELIEVING

These amazing illusions reveal the science behind the way we see. It's not just your eyes that see, but also your brain. It tries to make sense of what your eyes detect, and sometimes gets it a bit wrong.

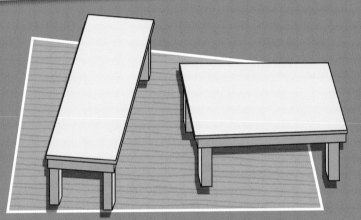

1. TABLETOPS
Which of these two tables is longer? Pretty obvious, right? Get a ruler and measure each tabletop's sides. You might be surprised.

Try each illusion out, and see if it works on your friends and family members, too.

TALK
TO THE
THE HAND

2. LINE SIZES
This well-known illusion is called the Ponzi illusion. Which pink line is the longest, or are they the same length? Measure them and see.

3. READ THE SIGN
This one's simple—just read the sign! What does it say?

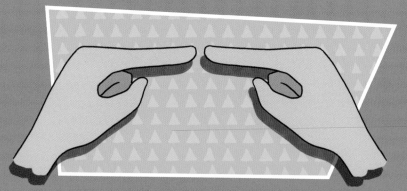

4. THE FLYING SAUSAGE

Hold your hands at arm's length, with your index fingers pointing toward each other, about ¼ inch (6 mm) apart, like this.

Now, look past your fingers at something far away. You should see a sausage form in midair between your fingertips!

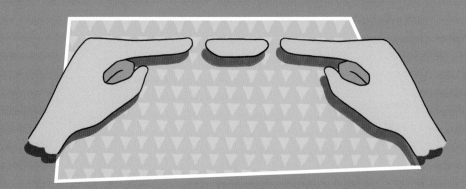

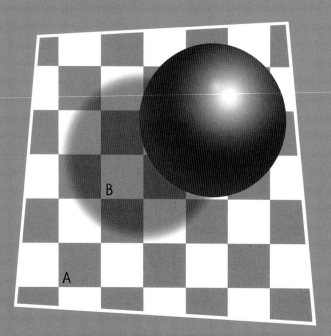

5. SHADOW SHADES

Look at the two squares marked A and B. Which one is the darker shade of gray?

HOW DO THEY WORK?

1. TABLETOPS: Because your brain interprets these images as three-dimensional, it sees them as long and short tables—even though the "short" one is actually longer than the "long" one.

2. LINE SIZES: The diagonal lines make you think one pink line is near and the other far away. If they were the same size, the faraway one should look smaller. As it doesn't, your brain decides it must be huge, when in fact it's slightly shorter than the "near" one.

3. READ THE SIGN: Did you spot the second "the"? Many people don't! The brain is often too busy to take in every little detail. Instead, it jumps to conclusions, and assumes things make sense.

4. THE FLYING SAUSAGE: Your eyes see the world from two slightly different angles. When you focus on something, you don't notice. But when you focus far away, the two different views of your fingers overlap each other, making the strange sausage shape.

5. SHADOW SHADES: Your brain judges how light or dark something is by its surroundings, so it thinks the square in the shadow must be lighter than the other one. In fact, they're both exactly the same shade, as you can see below.

TOUCH TRICKERY

Optical illusions aren't the only kind. There are also tactile illusions, which confuse your brain about what you can feel. Try these!

Try each illusion out and test them on friends and family. You'll need a helper for some of them.

1. THE TWO-NOSE ILLUSION

Cross your first and second fingers over each other, as far as they can go. Then use them to touch and feel the tip of your nose. It feels as if you have two noses! It works with other round objects, too, such as a marble.

2. THE LONG NOSE ILLUSION

For this, you need a friend who doesn't mind you touching their nose, and two chairs. Ask them to sit right in front of you. Shut your eyes, and use one hand to touch your own nose. Reach your other hand forward, and touch your friend's nose, using the exact same movements. It will feel as if their nose is yours, and your nose is really long!

3. FLOATING ARMS

Stand in a doorway, lift your arms out to your sides, and push the backs of your hands against the doorframe. Keep pushing them as hard as you can for about a minute. Then step away from the doorway and relax. Your arms will seem to magically float upward!

4. SILENT CHALK

Use a piece of chalk to write or scribble on a blackboard—or, if you don't have a blackboard, a sidewalk or patio. Then put in some earplugs or earphones playing music, or ask a friend to cover your ears. Try using the chalk again. It should feel much smoother!

HOW DO THEY WORK?

1. THE TWO-NOSE ILLUSION: It's very rare for the outside edges of your first and second fingers to be touching the same round object. The brain ignores your fingers being crossed, and instead decides that the fingers must be touching two different surfaces.

2. THE LONG NOSE ILLUSION: Your brain knows where your body parts are in space—so it knows your arm is far away from your face. But because both hands can feel a nose, it gets confused, and thinks your nose must be really long.

3. FLOATING ARMS: As the brain keeps sending the signal to lift your arms, it stops thinking about it, and starts sending the signal automatically. When you step away, the signal keeps going, even though you are not trying to lift your arms—and makes them seem to lift by themselves.

4. SILENT CHALK: The brain uses information from other senses to help it understand touch sensations. When you write with chalk, the scraping sound adds to the experience, making it feel rougher. Without the sound, it feels different!

ANT CAFÉ

To do this experiment, you'll need to first find an ants' nest. If you spot ants in your yard, park, or playground, you can set up this experiment close to where you've seen them.

WHAT YOU'LL NEED:

* ★ Three sticky notes (or just use paper and clear tape)
* ★ A ruler
* ★ A pen
* ★ Plain white sugar
* ★ Brown sugar
* ★ Artificial sweetener powder
* ★ A teaspoon
* ★ An ants' nest

(!) ASK AN ADULT!

1. Set up your experiment close to an ants' nest. If you can't find a nest, place it where you can see, or have seen, ants walking around or coming out of the ground.

Keep well away from the ants and don't bother them or touch them. Have an adult nearby.

2. Put the ruler on the ground and stick the three sticky notes along it. Bend them down slightly so that they lie flat against the ground.

3. Put a teaspoonful of white sugar on one note, a teaspoonful of brown sugar on another, and a teaspoonful of artificial sweetener on the third. Label each note with the type of food that is on it.

You could use a video camera or smartphone to record the ants feeding. Speeding the video up afterward will let you see quickly where the ants spent the most time.

4. Wait and watch to see if the ants come to your café. Which foods do they visit the most, and which the least?

HOW DOES IT WORK?

Ants seek out high-calorie food to give them energy. Sugar has a lot of calories, so it's usually very popular with ants. They may taste the artificial sweetener, but they can tell it doesn't contain as many calories, so they prefer the real sugar. Do they prefer one type of sugar to another? If so, this may be to do with the size of the grains, and how easy the sugar is to move and eat.

THE YEAST BALLOON

Yeast is a living thing, but it's not a plant or an animal. It's a type of fungus, and is related to mushrooms and mold. This balloon experiment lets you collect the gas that yeast makes as it grows.

WHAT YOU'LL NEED:

* An empty small plastic drink bottle
* A funnel
* Active dried yeast
* Sugar
* A teaspoon
* Hot water from the faucet
* A balloon
* (!) ASK AN ADULT!

1. Drop a teaspoon of dried yeast into the bottle, using the funnel. Then add a teaspoon of sugar, and shake the bottle around a bit to mix them together.

2. Ask an adult to add medium-hot water from the faucet to the bottle, to a depth of about 1 inch (2.5 cm). Gently shake and swirl the bottle to mix the water in.

4. Leave the bottle in a warm place, such as a sunny windowsill or near a radiator, and watch what happens.

3. Blow up the balloon to stretch it, then let it down again. Then stretch it over the neck of the bottle.

HOW DOES IT WORK?

Dried yeast is made up of lots of yeast cells. These are single-celled organisms that are much too small to see. When they get warm water and food (the sugar), they become "active", and start to feed and grow. As the yeast feeds on the sugar and turns it into energy, it makes bubbles of carbon dioxide gas as waste. You can see the bubbles forming in the mixture. As they pop, the gas starts to fill the bottle and the balloon.

When yeast is added to bread dough, the carbon dioxide bubbles make the dough rise and fill the bread with spaces, which makes it soft and squashy.

MEMORY TEST

Some things are easy to learn and remember, and others are much harder—people's memories don't always work very well! Try this memory test and see how well you do.

WHAT YOU'LL NEED:

* A dish towel
* A pen and paper
* A stopwatch or timer
* A tray
* At least one other person to be the tester
* A selection of ten different everyday objects, such as a key, a pen, a nail, toys, candies, a glove, a phone, a table tennis paddle, a tape measure, and so on.

1. The tester should collect all the objects together without you seeing them. They should just pick whatever objects they have at hand, and which are roughly the same size.

2. The tester should place the objects on a tray or table, and then hide them by covering them with the dish towel.

3. Now sit at the table with your pen and paper to take the test. Using the timer, the tester should remove the dish towel and show you the objects for ten seconds, before covering them up again. Then, the tester should give you one minute to write down all the objects you can remember.

4. Take off the dish towel and see how many you got right. Which ones did you remember first? Which did you forget?

HOW DOES IT WORK?

This game tests your short-term memory, which you use for storing things you've just experienced. People store memories more easily if they make them feel emotions. So, if you LOVE chocolate, you're likely to remember a chocolate bar. If you're scared of spiders, a plastic spider will stick in your brain. Look at your results and see if this was true for you.

You can test lots of different things with this experiment. For example, you could test people of different ages, and see who has the best memory. Or try testing your memory in the morning and at bedtime—when does it work best?

GLOSSARY

calorie A unit that is used to measure energy.

carbon dioxide A gas that is colorless and doesn't smell. It is a very small part of the air we breathe.

cell One of the tiny units from which all living things are made.

excrete To produce waste matter.

fungus A small organism that forms part of a larger group including yeasts and mushrooms.

illusion When the brain misinterprets the information it receives from the senses.

lactic acid A substance that is produced in the muscles during exercise and from lack of oxygen.

oxygen A gas that is essential for life.

respire To breathe.

sensation The physical feeling that is the result of sensing something.

FURTHER INFORMATION

Books

Amson-Bradshaw, Georgia. *Science In A Flash: Living Things*. London, UK: Franklin Watts, 2017.

Claybourne, Anna. *Whizzy Science: Make It Grow!* London, UK: Wayland Publishing, 2014.

Hutchinson, Sam. *Science Activity Book*. London, UK: b small publishing, 2016.

Mould, Steve. *How To Be A Scientist*. London, UK: DK Children, 2017.

Usborne Publishing. *365 Science Activities*. London, UK: Usborne Publishing, 2014.

Websites

http://www.sciencekids.co.nz/experiments.html
A whole host of experiments that let you explore the world of science.

https://youtu.be/AMvEVnAFCNA
This video shows you how to change the color of a flower's petals!

https://www.exploratorium.edu/snacks/subject/mechanics
Discover great experiments that explore optical illusions.

INDEX